D1397645

Hats in VOGUE

Hats
in
VOGUE

SINCE 1910

by Christina Probert

ABBEVILLE PRESS · PUBLISHERS · NEW YORK

ACKNOWLEDGMENTS

So many people have shared their talents with *Vogue* over the years: artists, photographers, designers, craftsmen, writers, but also *Vogue's* own editors whose perspicacious choices have shaped the magazine. I am grateful to Frederick Fox who was most generous with his time and information about the millinery world. I am indebted to Alex Kroll, Editor of Condé Nast Books, for his guidance throughout, Georgina Boosey for her editorial wisdom, Liz Bauwens for the book's design, Anna Houghton for her patience in coping with pictorial and editorial hurdles.

C.P.

First published in Great Britain by Thames and Hudson
in association with British *Vogue*

© 1981 by The Condé Nast Publications Ltd.
First published in the USA in 1981 by Abbeville Press, Inc.

All rights reserved under International and Pan-American Copyright Conventions. No part of this book may be reproduced or utilized in any form or by any means, electronic or mechanical, including photocopying, recording, or by any information storage and retrieval system, without permission in writing from the Publisher. Inquiries should be addressed to Abbeville Press, Inc., 505 Park Avenue, New York 10022. Printed and bound in Japan.

Library of Congress Cataloging in Publication Data
Main entry under title:

Hats in Vogue since 1910.

(Accessories in Vogue)
1. Hats—History—20th century.   2. Head-gear—History—20th century.
3. Millinery—History—20th century.   4. Vogue—History—20th century.
I. Probert, Christina.   II. Vogue.
GT2110.H33   391'.43'0904   81-14922
ISBN 0-89659-267-7 (pbk.)   AACR2

Cover. BV 1980 John Swannell. *Philip Somerville.* Back cover. FV 1924. *Lewis.* Page 2. GV 1980 John Stember. *Stephen Bruce.*

CONTENTS

Key to captions

Information is given in the following order: edition; artist or photographer;
designer or maker (the last always in *italic*). Editions are identified by initials:

A v American *Vogue*
B v British *Vogue*
F v French *Vogue*
G v German *Vogue*

INTRODUCTION

'Where did you get that hat?
Where did you get that tile?
Isn't it a nobby one and just the proper style?
I should love to have one just the same as that!
Where'er I go they shout "Hello!
Where did you get that hat?"'

James Rolmaz

Vastly flattering: oversized felt hat, its side 'à retroussis' to emphasize the mass of hair. Characteristic of the time, the downy ostrich feathers are almost as imposing as the hat itself.
A V 1910

The smartest hats have always been recherché. A Paris hat was every fashionable woman's desire at the turn of the twentieth century, a model created with the intangible flair of the French modiste. 'Go to Reboux looking tired, dejected,' suggested French *Vogue* in 1924, 'and you'll return happy and delighted – the ugly become beautiful, or at least that is the illusion, which is half the battle.' Naturally this handmade, unique (but oh so flattering) confection was expensive and thus attained the snob value which Rolmaz noted; it was a fashionable and social headstart. In choosing a hat, considerations like the time of day at which it is to be worn, practicality, price, the dictates of etiquette, climate and season, all pale into insignificance by comparison with the aura which a beautiful hat can create. The aura may be one of beauty, or merely of self-confidence, but it is this which has continued to make hats an important fashion accessory; a hat can catch any mood, match any style of dressing, while the rules of etiquette and custom change continually. 'To be just to oneself,' admitted British *Vogue* in 1918, 'one should be biased in the matter of hats.'

It has always been considered chic for one's hat to be individual, while maintaining the current look. Now, when the majority of hats are no longer 'models', the embarrassment of encountering an identical hat at Royal Ascot has become more probable. In other areas of hat-wearing the opposite is the case: for schools, police, similarity is the vital factor to emphasize group characters, not those of the constituent individuals.

The history of hats is long and varied. For centuries they have been sartorial status symbols: visible signs of wealth, religion, nationality, political beliefs, occupation. At times when communications between and within

1910

A whole stuffed owl ornaments this wide straw. A V 1910. *Burgesser.*

The fashionable mourner, in tiny white poke bonnet with yards of black crepe. A V 1917

countries were difficult, such symbols helped to identify outsiders. In the Roman Empire, to be crowned with a laurel wreath was a mark of respect for heroism; aristocratic ladies wore jewelled headdresses which, as marks of birth and standing, symbols of wealth, changed according to fashion. In Renaissance Italy the retinues of the leading families wore distinctive hats, of individual colour and design for each house, as visible reminders of their power, patronage, politics and wealth. Hats also have religious symbolism: the Pharaohs' headdresses had mystical significance; ecclesiastics today wear hats to display their rank and faith. There are widely held theories that the shape of hats changes with, and even forecasts, the social, political and economic climate. As a women's fashion accessory, hats continue to play a significant role; in 1910 etiquette demanded that hats should be worn out of doors, whatever the weather and the time of day, and often indoors too. Now, when hats need be worn only on formal occasions, they are generally worn as a matter of personal choice, in style, size and colour tempered only by the dictates of current make-up, hair and dress fashion.

At the end of the nineteenth century, fashionable hats were generally small, perched high on the head, dominated aesthetically by the clumps of false hair which every smart woman wore; alternatively, bonnets were large enough to engulf the whole coiffure. As the silhouette became less bolstered, skirts narrower, hair more natural, hats began to increase in size and visual importance. *Vogue* reflected the great emphasis on millinery, running extensive editorials on new styles, for example 'Tracing Some of Our Recent Feminine Headgear to Queer Sources' in August 1909, which found tribal and national prototypes for fashionable shapes. Since the smartest hats were made to measure, *Vogue* ran a regular column called 'Vogue Points for Milliners', detailing the construction and ornamentation of a selection of new hats.

During the second decade of the twentieth century, hat styles changed fast and dramatically. Radical changes were taking place in the way in which women dressed: corsets became softer, less bulky, clothes too. Skirts shortened to reveal the long-hidden shoes, but the hat remained stable, unchanged in function or basic construction. It was fashion's emblem, its centrepiece, as it developed from season to season.

In 1909 emphasis was on the crown of the hat: turbans were created for day and evening, with or without brims, in two or three toning fabrics, with floral decoration. Pleated and folded swathes of rich-coloured and textured fabrics formed berets. Soft 'Rembrandt' hats had wide brims, as did firmer summer styles of straw and tulle. French millinery terms gave the Paris touch: a cone-shaped hat with flattened crown covered in velvet was the 'Chasseur d'Afrique' hat, for it resembled the hats worn by the French army in Morocco, 'peau de rat' was a pliable felt, feathers were 'gorge de pigeon', 'canard sauvage'. In 1910 hats were vast, the shape traditionally worn by Little Miss Muffet: a crown so high and broad that it appeared perpetually in danger of falling over the wearer's eyes. The whole confection, of leghorn and lace for summer, glazed straw, chip for winter, was ornamented further by huge bunches of roses, whole stuffed birds, feathers, whose arrangement changed subtly and frequently. Velvet, moiré, lace, satin and tulle were new alternatives to the ever-popular straws. The 'ruban de toile ciré' was the latest ornamentation, a straw ribbon with glazed finish, also moiré, taffeta, velvet or faille ribbons which replaced satin.

By the outbreak of the Great War the whole mood of hat design was changing. There was a new vertical emphasis which superseded the broad, rather heavy style of earlier hats. Fanciful names continued to be given to the smartest shapes and materials: the 'tête de nègre' straw crown had a 'fancy ostrich feather burned out to make it delicate'; the 'Chapeau Niniche' was a bandeau hat raised at the back and towards the side, ornamented with flowers and ribbons. Evening shapes, too, emphasized the hair: in 1914 coloured wigs, in mauve, green, white were the latest thing when worn with a bejewelled and befeathered bandeau. In wartime fine lace veils of varying lengths came into fashion; American *Vogue* in 1917 showed French hats and veils 'designed to console very young widows . . . for the Parisienne never altogether lays aside her coquetry. She can not. It is inborn.'

'One of the newest hats' said British *Vogue* in 1917, 'is a *cloche* designed by Lucie Hamar'. This earliest version looked very unlike its twenties sisters: it had a tall crown widening to the summit, a large brim. This brim was very versatile, it could be pinned up at front or side, or even back, or could be turned down to shade the eyes with the addition of a veil. 'Ever so many hats are one-sided affairs,' said *Vogue* in 1918, 'on the right side of course.'

Colours, fabrics and trimmings for hats varied enormously between 1910 and 1920. At first plain colours with brightly contrasting trimmings were used, one colour being promoted each season. Fur was always a popular winter addition to hats. Later in the decade printed and embroidered fabrics, lace, dotted net, moiré, velvet, silk, tulle, faille, crin and taffeta became alternatives to felt and to the myriad straws, varying from coarse chip to the finest lace-woven variety. Smartest ornaments in 1909 were feathers in long swathes, particularly ostrich and écume feathers (which were very fine indeed), voluminous rosettes of Malines tulle, straggly squirrel tail aigrettes and plaited silk, soft velvet. Later, flowers were used, whole stuffed birds, ribbons. By the end of the decade ornament had become less overpowering, supplementary to the hats' design, except for parties, when they were laden with miniature pagodas, flower-baskets, jewel boxes. 'A great change has come about in the buying of hats,' noted *Vogue*: 'it is the new idea to choose a hat solely on account of its decorative effect.'

Party hat.
A V 1919
Turban with ostrich feather 'burned out'.
A V 1914 Helen Dryden.
Valentine About

The cloche in 1917, satin faced with straw. B V 1917. *Lucie Hamar*

1920

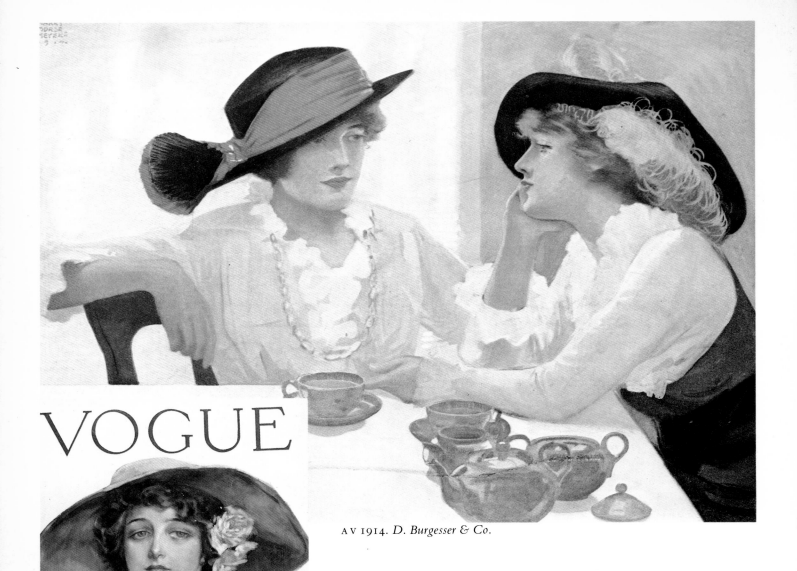

VOGUE

AV 1914. *D. Burgesser & Co.*

AV 1911 Z. P. Nikolaki

A very informal straw, the most popular material for hats, *this page left*. With roses under the brim, and long ties to ward off breezes, it was ideal for a summer afternoon spent reading in the garden. Two afternoon hats, *above*, worn with the highly fashionable lingerie blouses which were as pretty and frilly as the bodice beneath. The hat on the right is a 'Rembrandt' shape, with ruff effect under the brim and curled feathers; the other is more formal, with high crown and firm brim. *Opposite* is an early antecedent of the hard hat. Rigidly constructed, it has the high, wide crown giving the falling-over-the-eyes look characteristic of the first decade of the century.

AV 1909 Vivien Valdaire

AV 1914

BV 1918 Campbell. *Valentine About*

Prints and lace were used for summer hats. The chintz hat with a pink lining, *above left*, 'has become very much involved in a pleasant and frivolous relationship with yards and yards of pink ribbon'. The shallow-crowned lace hat, *above*, matches the skeleton front of lace which Doucet gave the dress 'as a compromise between the dictates of fashion and modesty'.

Five smart hats of 1917, lighter in
weight and trimming, younger at heart.
Three have vertical emphasis, in a
whirling drapery of velvet *above left*, in
ostrich-quill antennae and varnished
quills *above and below right*. Newly
popular, too, was the low-crowned
picture hat: in straw *centre*, and faille
silk *below left,* both lightly trimmed
with glacé silk flowers (black poinsettias).

BV 1917 Helen Dryden. *Waters & Co.*

AV 1917 E.O. Hoppé

Mrs John Lavery, in a vast satin cape with wide fur collar, and one of the latest breed of small hats, made from crocodile-, snake- and lizardskin, with a tiny veil folded around the hair shading the eyes.

BV 1919 De Meyer

Lady Ribblesdale, in a velvet coat with fur collar. Her hat, in dark brocade, has a low crown, the brim
turned down at the front, up at the back, with a huge knot of fine feathers on top.

B V 1917 De Meyer

A V 1917 De Meyer. *Lewis*

B V 1916

B V 1918

B V 1918

AV 1911

The changing mood of millinery from 1911 to 1918. *On this page* are two flowery hats: *above* of rough straw bound with satin ribbon, flower print fabric and finished with a cluster of tiny roses at the side, and *on the right* a yellow felt with pink roses and a huge black and white striped bow. By 1916 lavish clumps of flowers had diminished or even disappeared; the Duchess of Marlborough's turban, *opposite centre*, is decorated only with a swathe of its own, very fashionable, ciré cotton. *Opposite above left and right*: two wide-brimmed hats from 1917, one of wired white net, covered with white crepe georgette dripping over the brim, the crown wreathed with pansies and cherries, the other of black horsehair braid trimmed with paradise feathers. The following year brought smaller brims into fashion: tan faille silk lined with dark blue, *opposite below left*, and black and white striped straw, with firm brim and black taffeta bow, *opposite below right*.

AV 1911. *Weiss*

A V 1919 George Plank

On the beach, *left*, tall yet tiny with a wide parasol to make up for its lack of shade. Almost an oval of shaped mauve felt, ornamented with cherries and ribbon bow, the hat is in keeping with the current long, slim silhouette, which Poiret had made fashionable. *Opposite* is another hat for a summer out-of-doors, although the clouds look threatening; it is decorated with dots under the brim, a simple ribbon around the crown. An amusing hat which is not just a flight of fantasy, *above*, drawn by George Plank, is a Japanese garden for the head, complete with tree: these hats were so popular for fancy-dress parties in 1919 that *Vogue* ran an article full of ideas such as pagoda hats, fruit-basket hats, jewel-box hats.

A V 1914 Helen Dryden   B V 1917 Helen Dryden

1920

Very soft leather, bloused cloche. B V 1926. *Rose Descat*

Crepe de chine cloche with Oriental embroidery. F V 1924. *Lanvin*

Cavalier hat in Musketeer style: black velours with silver ribbon. B V 1923. *Lewis*

'Certain it is,' said British *Vogue* in 1923, 'that the modistes wish a change in millinery modes, for during the last three years we have worn the same shapes without caring to alter them . . . Reboux protests against the cloche.' Traditionally acclaimed as the hat of the twenties, the cloche had, in fact, been introduced in 1917: a brimmed hat with tall crown widening to a flattened summit. Gradually, however, 'cloche' came to mean any small, close-fitting hat with or without a small brim, usually with a rounded crown. Milliners tired of the continuing demand for the same type of hat, tried in vain to oust the cloche family by creating new, totally different looks. In vain, because this neat, streamlined hat had captured the mood in the early twenties, when fashion was sports- and practicality-orientated. This mood permeated every level of society, provoking a vendeuse, in 1923, to beg the Comtesse de Moustiers 'not to choose the cloche . . . it is so *midinette*!'

The cloche was not, however, the only fashionable hat in the twenties. There were cloche derivatives, with wide, soft brims; neat hats with draped crowns; brimless styles. In addition there were turbans, toques, hats with balloon crowns, berets, boaters. *Vogue* noted that women's millinery choice was 'no longer dependant on the charming aspect of a hat, but on the harmonious general effect of the silhouette.'

In the early twenties variety lay in use of trimmings, colours and materials. Hats had a summer garden feel in 1920 and 1921: flower colours, garland decoration, finding their 'perfect setting in the green of an English lawn'. Others were swathed with lace, tulle, netting, to soften the line of the hat as it changed to its new small shape. Crowns were often draped folds of fabric, or peaked, but the vertical emphasis, so important in the previous decade, was diminishing. Summer hats, sometimes in semi-transparent straw or tulle, had drooping brims and feathers. Etiquette, as far as use of fabric was concerned, was changing: 'Neither warm weather nor formal occasions prevent the smart Parisienne from appearing in a felt hat and a summer fur.'

The film world affected hats: in 1923 the screening of *The Three Musketeers* made the Musketeer style fashionable. Other theatrical effects were achieved with beads, silver tissue, tulle, cabochons, spangles, ornaments mounted on a scrap of velvet or a fillet. Hairstyles were shaped to match the whole look, concealing the ears 'lost in a mystery of curls or hat or headdress'. By 1924 the cloche was restrictingly low, and brims began to be turned up at front and back to enable the wearer to see out and move her head. By 1925 the brim, or absence of it, had become a focal point; some were swept back, halo-like, some cut, twisted, folded. The toque was now top news. It was an ideally simple canvas for Art Deco ornamentation, for the achievement of 'simplicity by complication', with appliqué and 3-D effects. The 1925 Paris Art Deco Exhibition had stimulated fashion design, and its influence on millinery is evident. Another trend reflected in *Vogue* was 'the cubistic manner': broken surfaces, mosaic motifs in textures as varied as velvets, shaved lamb, satin. Madame Agnès' models, particularly, reflected this relationship between fashion and the decorative arts. The turban (especially for evening) and the toque outstripped brimmed hats in popularity.

Colour combinations and a plain ribbon were the only ornamentation on 1926's smartest hats. Recent fashions for lace, aigrettes and cabochons seemed antiquated, for simplicity was now the prime consideration in styling and trimming. The newest focal point was the crown, blousing out and growing taller each season. The firm felts and leathers used were made to appear soft and supple. The toque continued to hold sway in 1927, tall, brimless, sometimes with pleated crown to match the fashionable pleated skirts, or geometric patterning. Worn with huge earrings for evening, smaller, rounded ones for day, just a suspicion of curl was allowed to escape at the sides. As hats with brims of uneven width appeared, tilted over the left eye, pinned up on one side, *Vogue* confirmed that 'Irregularity has become the rule.' By the third quarter of the twenties wider brims were worn: 'the large summer hat can no longer figure as a "strictly American" fashion, for Paris has accepted it'; those with drooping brims were called 'semi-large' hats.

An enormous variety of straws and fabrics was used during the twenties. Each year the predominant medium changed, providing the up-to-date look while hat shapes remained rather static. Satin in 1920 was followed by crepe de chine, popular for four fashion seasons, together with lace, tulle, tissue, velvet, fine straws, crepe georgette, leghorn. The year 1923 saw a revival of the plain Milan straws, such as that treated to look like satin, picot, a straw called 'pedaline' which was a mixture of Cellophane and raw straw. By mid-decade there was a move towards velvets, furs, and to felt, which dominated the decade. Straws were popular from 1928, also taffeta hats.

Ornamentation was particularly lively during the first and last quarters of the decade, colours always varied and exciting. Swathes of net and tulle, ribbon-bound edges, embroidery, silver lace, clusters of ciré fruits and flowers, green imitation grass straw strips, were all very popular. Feathers, too, were highly fashionable essentials, a 'ragged rain of ospreys' for brims, small aigrettes, glycerinized ostrich feathers, and, above all, cock's feathers, particularly 'coq de roche'. Mid-decade, there were greens, greys, browns and beige, simple ribbons or painted decoration on the body of the hat. In 1927 yellow hats were the rage, often with white, also pink, burgundy, black, beige, bois de rose; the following year added hyacinth, jungle-green, scarlet, blue, to the now extensive list of wearable colours. Detail was contained in the hat itself in the form of tucks, pleats, slits in crown and brim.

The austerity of hats in the middle twenties had, by 1930, disappeared in favour of a soft summery look described by *Vogue*: 'Nothing in nature or art is so magically transforming as a wide drooping hat of summer lightness'.

3-D appliqué in Art Deco style. FV 1925. *Agnès*

Summer-garden, lacy hat *above*, that *right* flamboyantly military. BV 1921. *Albert (right)*

1930

B V 1926 Porter Woodruff

A V 1927 Harriet Meserole

Some of the fashionable millinery styles of the twenties, all characterized by their simplicity of effect, although many, such as that *above*, were of complicated construction. The lady with fashionably short curly hair, *opposite*, is busy examining her purchases for the spring season. She holds up a stone felt toque, with green satin ribbon trimming, and a high-crowned (very smart at this time) wide-brimmed felt with dark brown trimmings – felt was equally popular for summer or winter. *On this page, above*, is an angular high-crowned cloche with a rouleau brim and ingeniously swathed crown. This broken surface and textured effect, like that of the huge straw *right*, was popular from the mid-twenties; these wide-brimmed hats became increasingly fashionable at the end of the decade. *Above right* is a triple view of a cloche with stripes as its theme, the brim shaped to disappearing point at the centre front.

B V 1925 Pierre Brissaud

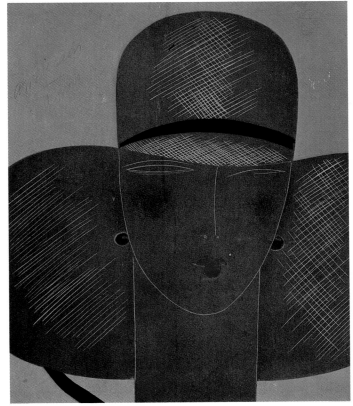

A V 1929 Benito

23

B V 1923 Douglas Pollard. *Rose Descat*

B V 1926 Benito. *Agnès*

The cloche, renamed 'the helmet' by milliners: *on the left* resembling a squared toque, in black and beige; *on the right* a 'turban', with fringed layers of tête de nègre grosgrain; in taffeta, *above*, with back brim and clipped ostrich trimming. The 'flower-pot' picot straw, *opposite*, has cock's feathers arranged to 'outdo the Modernist at his own game'.

B V 1926 Benito. *Reboux*

B V 1922 Helen Dryden. *Reboux*

BV 1928 Benito

During the second half of the twenties small hats clung more tightly than ever to the head; many were brimless. The influence of Art Deco was evident in hat shapes, ornamentation, colouring, and even in hairstyles. This yellow felt hat, *left*, worn with brown, camel and yellow print scarf, has a corresponding geometric glass cabochon at one side. The lop-sided look was a smart one, too, and is echoed in the hat *opposite*, with its brim turned up only on one side. The body of the hat is felt, pin-tucked for a textured effect, with a taffeta ribbon brim. A diamanté bar completes the modern look, glinting as brightly as the surrounding neons.

BV 1927 Lepape

'Mrs Cochrane Bailey, looking refreshingly cool and comfortable in a chiffon dress, takes a stroll with Lord Portarlington.'

Above: 'Mrs Maurice Kingscote, whose husband is a cousin of Mr Nigel Kingscote, of Kingscote, in a black toilette and picture hat.'
Right: 'Lady Montagu of Beaulieu and Lady Sinclair about to go aboard Lord Montagu's yacht at Cowes.'

'A summer snapshot of the Countess of Pembroke, whose only daughter, Lady Patricia Herbert, attains her majority this year.'

'Bonnets, berets, Dolly Vardons, toques, Homburgs, Lancrets, tammies, sailors, vagabonds, pictures, Zouaves, mephistopheles-caps, skull-helmets: these are some of the types of hat that are worn by the crowd. Felt hats, straw hats, hard, bendy, glossy, mat, flowered, untrimmed, moulded, draped, pink hats, blue hats, white, scarlet and yellow hats are to be seen in the Park, at Church and at Ascot, and so great is the variety that one wonders how the wearers have come to make their own final decision; one wonders how their taste has been formed, by whom or what they have been influenced and by what channels their fancy has run riot in this or that direction. . . . Why that glycerined straw bonnet bedecked generously with variegated country flowers, trembling grasses and lapis-lazuli butterflies? . . . Why the hollow grapes, why the chimney pot? . . . Here is a cross-section of the more heavily hatted.' (Cecil Beaton.)

BV 1928 Cecil Beaton

1930

Almost crownless, perched 'smack over the forehead' was the 'coup de vent' hat. FV 1935. *Talbot*

The cloche: now the traditional sports hat in soft felt. BV 1931 Hoyningen-Huené. *Rose Valois*

Fantasy was one of the strongest elements in the innovative and exciting hats of the decade: 'the new season's hats', said French *Vogue* in 1935, 'never fail to put a spring in the already gay, fantasy-laden air'. Women wore 'ingratiatingly frivolous' hats, modelled on Arcadian shepherds' hats, Persian turbans, Henri III hats. New and crazy interpretations of traditional styles, new ideas, appeared throughout the decade, for 'no hat ever invented is safe from the smart woman casting around for fresh sources of supply – not the exclusive, professional headgear of a soldier, sailor (tinker, tailor), dustman, chef, bull-fighter, or cowboy.' The chameleon politics and economics of the thirties were reflected in fashionable hats, there was an uncanny leaning towards military styles trimmed with cockades, the bicorne, tricorne, peaked cap – for, as *Vogue* noted, hat creators are an accurate, swift barometer of mood.

Whereas the clothes of the twenties had exposed the body for the first time since the early nineteenth century, those of the thirties flattered it. Hats now revealed the head itself, not just the shape of the cranium enclosed in tight-fitting helmet, and the neck, ears, hair. 'All smart hair is longer,' said *Vogue* in 1930, 'but long hair is not smart.' As the decade progressed, styles grew higher and gained breadth, the soft chignon came back into fashion in a soft form, high and broad, forming a platform for the 'puppet-size' hats which were perched on top.

An active interest in sports, which became a part of every woman's life in the thirties, created the vogue for the sports hat. Soft-crowned, soft-brimmed, it varied in minor details but never mood, which was the most casual yet seen in millinery during the century. At the beginning of the decade its chief rival was the small, neat hat, as *Vogue* noted: 'the trim, young, chipper hats that Paris is making are the perfect solution.' Both types were 'masculine', with sombre colouring and plain trimming; masculine too was the 'most gigantic sailor [hat] . . . seen for four years . . . the hat sensation of 1932 . . . hat of hats to wear after four o'clock.' Feminine rivals were the leghorn, 'very big, very smart, the old favourite of the Parisiennes . . . from the days of real flirtations', and the multitude of fantasy hats which had begun to appear in every shape and fabric.

By mid-decade the crown and brim were still locked in their traditional fight for supremacy, 'just like two great families, Montague and Capulet, the two are always rivals . . . just now the brim triumphs . . . the crown shrivels away as if exposed to heat' (French *Vogue*, 1935). Many hats were almost crownless, flat as a plate, with brims sloping down over the forehead. There were adaptations of the mortar-board with curled edges, soft shallow sports hats with indented crowns, in chamois, felts. But despite French *Vogue*'s protestations that the crown was out of favour, both British and American *Vogues* showed brimless conical hats and Paris adopted them by the end of the year. The conical hat remained popular until 1938: treatment of the shape varied from veiled velvet to black felt, with a white cockade standing to attention. The varied hats in fashion in the second half of the decade had one overriding feature in common: they were 'perched smack over the forehead, on rising levels of hair'. *Vogue* advised readers to 'tilt hats with abandon, over your nose or ears, spring "sailors" are meant to be cock-eyed.' The new breed of hat with curled, folded, pleated, winged effects relied on superb technique: in felt or firm straw, portions of the brim were cut and caught up, or sewn in graduated layers to create an angular, stark look. The boater continued to be worn, sometimes with heightened crown, or in fabric with pinned up brim. Most sought after were 'hats so small they scarcely cover a single curl' created by milliners and couturiers alike: 'Schiaparelli's toy-sized toppers', for example, 'look as if they might have been a party favour, little flat plates about the size of a poker chip, a bunch of flowers mounted on elastic': tiny, shiny, pork-pie hats for autumn, piqué clusters of daisies, leaves, bows, feathers, a pinwheel scattering veils for summer. Ornament and veiling were key factors, adding still more colour to the hat.

Fabric, colour and decoration of millinery varied tremendously from beginning to end of the thirties. At the outset colours were sombre: greys, browns, wine-red, black with green, white, oranges, amber for summer. Matt and shiny fabrics were fashionable: felt, rough straws, varnished straw in black, white, natural. Mid-decade softer fabrics appeared, silk and rayon jersey, broadcloth, velvet, flannel, chenille, taffeta. Bright-coloured feathers were clustered high on the head as a hat, or used as decoration. *Vogue* said 'You'll be preening your plumage, this autumn – what with feathers on practically every other hat.' Puffs of velvet, chenille, silks and prints were gathered at the side of the head. From mid-decade black was smart at every occasion, in every fabric. Pale colours and primaries abounded, adorned with the 'flowers which continue to enchant the milliners . . . used in unprecedented ways.' The new element was the veil, always in evidence, but now used in a 'soft, often brightly coloured way . . . there is nothing more flattering, which does more for the facial structure.' The euphoric mood of fashion immediately prior to the outbreak of the Second World War, as national economies pulled out of the Depression, seems, with hindsight, like a rather sad Indian summer. American *Vogue* summed up the mood of exuberant hat design: 'Put nothing between your hair and the breeze but a hat as small as a doll's. Let a bunch of flowers anchored to your head with elastic pass for a hat. Wind up your head in a length of wool mesh and fasten it with a clip or a flower . . . mantillas, peasant kerchiefs, ostrich feathers, etc., anything goes'.

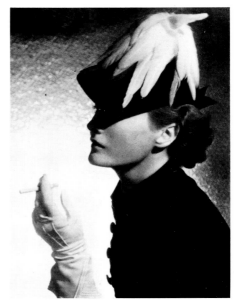

Cavalry plumed cone foreshadows the war. BV 1935 Horst. *Agnès*

'Toy-size toppers', with frills, bows. AV 1938 Eric. *Schiaparelli, Bruyère*

1940

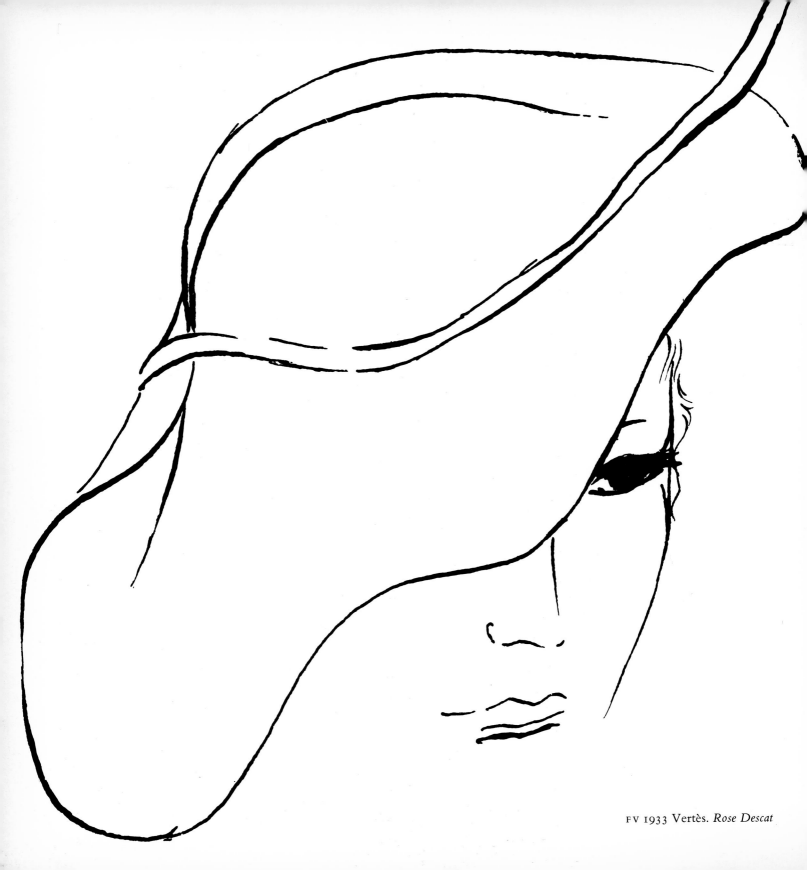

FV 1933 Vertès. *Rose Descat*

Celebrating the temporary
victory of brim over crown in
the lifelong battle for
supremacy are these two almost
crownless hats, soft in fabric
and in the undulation of their
brims. The angle at which they
are worn is merely a
conservative foreshadow of that
fashionable later in the decade.
The spring felt *opposite* has a
mere suggestion of a brim
blocked from the single plate of
felt which sweeps down over
one eye. *On this page* is a more
formal velvet version modelled
by Miss Koopman, who
appeared on one of *Vogue*'s
earliest photographic covers.

BV 1934 Beaton. *Geene Glenny*

FV 1939 Bouché. *Suzy*

AV 1936 Willaumez. *Suzy*

FV 1939 Eric. *Agnès*

Many hats were planted with flowers during the second half of the thirties, so much so that Suzy's hat shop, *above left*, looks like a summer garden in full bloom. Crownlessness was still the mode in 1936; *above*, the hat in the foreground is merely a rough straw brim with a garland of shiny leaves and nasturtiums. Behind it are a 'couronne' of hydrangeas on a tiny skull cap and an organza oval, flat as a plate, with three long-stemmed tulips as decoration. By the end of the decade the crown had returned to fashion, for hats large and small: *left*, a rough straw for casual summer wear, *above left*, a selection of the fashionable tiny hats, and larger shapes, too, with squared crowns, masses of feathers, frills, flowers.

Despite the frivolous small hats, there were
still very big, very smart hats in fashion. The hat *on
this page* is of parrabuntel straw, a light, flexible, shiny
type, which reappeared as a fashionable material in the seventies.

BV 1936

FV 1936 Landshoff. *Maria Guy*

BV 1936 Miles. *Harrods*

Some of the folded, twisted, angled breed of hats, demonstrating the skill of their creators. This type of hat was known as a beret, despite dissimilarity to its traditional namesake, and was worn with the newly long hairstyles, draped into neat rolls or curls at the back. The draped black beret, *opposite*, is of heavy felt, with small, fine veil over the eyes; *on this page* are two more versions in straw, that *above left* a very shiny type, while that *above right* is a matt green straw which resembles toile. Tallulah Bankhead, *right*, wears another hat on swept-up lines, in black felt with a long feather trim.

Overleaf: two fashion fantasies based on traditional hats. A corsair felt, *left*, and a mortar-board pinioned with a pirate's bandanna, *right*.
BV 1936 Eric. *Suzy, Agnès*

FV 1936 Pagès. *Louise Bourbon*   AV 1939 Horst

FV 1939 Blumenfeld.
Legroux Soeurs

FV 1939 Blumenfeld. *Rose Valois*

Euphoria on the Eiffel Tower: two shots, *on this page*, from Blumenfeld's magnificent sitting just before the war overshadowed fashion. The hats are playful too. *Opposite* is a very sophisticated boater, in bengal straw with a spiralling straw ribbon, 'Black Prince' roses as ornamentation: *on this page below* is another boater, but in this case a toy-sized veiled one in rough straw, with the brim raised at either side and a tiny bird with long tail prostrated on it. *On the right* is a circular brimless hat, with a large cluster of ribbon at one side, worn at a revealingly rakish angle.

FV 1939 Blumenfeld. *Rose Valois*

FV 1939. *Agnès*

AGNÈS

The veil at its most seductive, most significant, as it bursts into colour, *opposite*. The tiny pinwheel toque, perched over the forehead, is circled by swathe after swathe of finest printed tulle. More veils, *on this page*, fashionably long, embroidered, with minute hats atop high hairstyles, the straw saucer on the left abloom with lilacs, the roll-brimmed straw on the right with chiffon veiling.

43

1940

Versatile day or evening
veiled hat. F V 1940 Bérard. *Erik*

Tiny-crowned fine straw. A V 1943

'The hat is not just an accessory, it is as important a marker of times and fashions as the length of skirts' (French *Vogue*, 1940). Wartime shortages and sartorial controls affected forties hats, but styles continued to evolve without the break in mood which occurred in most other fashion areas. Hats were a special case, for they became women's banner of individuality, of continued attention to appearance, morale-boosters. As French *Vogue* noted, shortly before its enforced closure: 'In our present austerity it is the hat which has to make the whole outfit, to remind women that they are young, that they must continue to look pretty; the hat has to enliven faces which have become serious.'

In the United States, as in Europe, small hats were the rule in wartime, rising even higher from the brow, which became a focal point. American versions were in luxury fabrics, velvet, satin, leather, suede, European ones in felt, dress fabric, coarse fabric covered in unrationed fabric flowers, braiding. After the war, although European models were once again imported, the American fashion industry built on its wartime foundations to produce indigenous model hats and clothes.

Unlike clothes, millinery recovered very swiftly from wartime restrictions. But although the New Look of 1947 brought large hats back into fashion, to balance the newly full skirts (not seen since the thirties), the small hat did not disappear. In 1949 American *Vogue* noted that 'the spring's new hats have developed rather than changed . . . the basis of them all is the little head with short, short hair.' Hairstyles altered more radically than hats during the decade. Permanent waves, smart since the thirties, and professional haircuts were rare luxuries in wartime. Thus longer hair came into fashion, in rolls around the head, particularly over the brow. This was achieved by wrapping the hair around rags or soft curlers overnight, or around a hairband in daytime, which the hair concealed. Pin-curls were smart too. After the war, hair fashions more reliant on professional treatments re-emerged, with the hat 'once more playing a leading role, the hair its brilliant understudy.

During the early forties *Vogue*'s millinery pages were still peppered with mini-hats. Worn at increasingly rakish angles, they leaned forward or to one side, sometimes with veiling attached to keep hair fashionably 'neat'. Two of the smartest shapes were the boater and Breton. The boater was adapted for wartime wear with a veil or paisley scarf built into the design, completely enfolding the head, or laden with unrationed flowers, particularly at the back: a focal point as hair lengthened. The Breton, described as 'an architectural beret' and as a 'backward beret', appeared in all sizes and fabrics, the brim folding sharply back, or sloping gently like a halo. 'Bretons are bigger', said American *Vogue* in 1940, 'in both senses, than ever.' American hats were designed to cling so tightly to the head that elastic was unnecessary;

British *Vogue*, meanwhile, showed hats consisting of little more than a cluster of flowers on a metal band.

By the last two years of the war the stocks of unrationed ribbon, flowers and feathers were running out. Hats were now made from scraps of fabric, stiffened fabric covered in braid, or felt. The beret, in woven and knitted fabric, was worn tilted over one eye; American versions were of satin, rayon velvet, quilting, some were brimmed. Hair underneath these draped to the neck, ending in a bun, chignon or roll. The capot, 'cunningly cut and shaped' over a frame, imitated these hairstyles. Turbans in various fabrics were popular: jersey, silk, cotton, in a puffed out or fitted form; American *Vogue* described them as 'a recurrent fashion, primitive and now again notable.' Developments on the theme produced hats apparently inflated from within, yet with no more substance than puffs of fabric mounted on frames, in silk, felt, satin.

That France had returned to the front line of fashion in 1946 is evident in the sudden influx of new hats on *Vogue*'s pages. The puff-of-fabric hat widened began to slant at forty-five degrees. All hats showed signs of the swept-up front, and were worn further back, for, as American *Vogue* said, 'the new chic is in how you shape the hat ... how you wear it'. The traditional boater developed a shaped brim, indented crown. Hats were structured again, the oversized, rose-laden styles of the early century were revived, and the broad, firmly built New Look hat appeared. This mood soon passed in favour of large hats with tucked-up brims, and soft-brimmed styles. By the end of the decade the small hat, with fine veiling draped around the head harem-style, had returned to fashion. Whatever its size, the angle to wear it at was at least forty-five degrees. The brow was now almost always visible, with hair kept back and up, and as a result make-up, used sparingly before the war, gained importance.

Colour, fabric and ornamentation of hats varied a great deal during the decade. European wartime hats were often garish, using as many fabric flowers, ribbons, braids as were available to brighten the often dull outfits. Turbans and scarves were made from fabric scraps. In the United States tropical bird colours were popular, in silk jersey, satin, quilted and waffled fabrics, rayon velvet. Feathers were popular, except during the latter war years when they were difficult to obtain. After the war, cock, pigeon and glycerinized ostrich feathers were revived. Straw was difficult to obtain in wartime, but fine straws in pastel colours with fine tulle-like brims returned to fashion after the war. 'The best hats,' said American *Vogue*, 'are not only lovely in themselves, they lend a new beauty to the women who wear them ... psychologically they are like a lovely smile. You can't see it in yourself, but you feel its effect in the eye of the beholder.'

Wartime economies: tiny saucer hats. A V 1943 Rawlings. *Hattie Carnegie, I Magnin*

Turban-derived summer hat turned back like a half Breton. A V 1947 Eric. *Sally Victor*

1950

B V 1946 Horst

Grand hats celebrate
the end of the war:
newly available
luxury fabrics and
handmade flowers
contribute to their
elegance. *On this
page* is a milk and
honey confection in
an Edwardian
mood, bound with
ribbons and laden
with full-blown
roses. In a more
sophisticated mood
is the puff-of-fabric
hat *opposite*, in
bright satin, worn
with long earrings
and upswept hair.

B V 1945 Rawlings

A V 1944 Rawlings.
Tatiana du Plessis

B V 1942 Horst. *Scotts*

B V 1944 Rawlings. *Erik*

The smaller, often brimless wartime
hat, seen on both sides of the
Atlantic. Both hats use generous
amounts of fabric: a swirl of satin on
the small toque, *opposite*, and a huge
billow of felt for the turban, *right*.
The restricted fabric allowance for
British hats is demonstrated by the
chéchia, *top*, cut economically from
several small pieces of felt, and by
the draped capot, *above*.

A V 1944 Rawlings. *Suzanne et Roger*

V 1941 Eric.
enri Bendel

Two black and warm-green creations, *opposite*, described by American *Vogue* as 'one of this autumn's most prettifying forms for hats – the romantic riding-hat.' Five years later the silhouette was still the same. The Balenciaga and Schiaparelli hats, *this page*, have the same tilt, are still visibly affected by shortage of materials, still create an elongated head shape, with the hair drawn back beneath them.

Schiaparelli's loop-hat

Balenciaga's plumed toque

Balenciaga's pill-box

B V 1946
Cecil Beaton

w 1948 Nepo. *Christian Dior*

The return of femininity to
fashion. A silk slip and chiffon
overdress, *on this page*, with
more fullness everywhere, and
a wide, tulle-edged hat,
foreshadow Dior's New Look
which arrived the following
year. And after the New Look:
a wide straw from Dior himself,
with feathers creating a brim
like a wing.

B V 1946 Penn

v 1948 Bouché.
Olga Mattli

After the diminutive and often rather severe hats of the early forties came the swathed, draped look. A sizeable toque, *opposite*, worn on top of still long but pinned-up hair, is draped with lacy veil to frame the face. Now that feathers were once again available, designers in Paris created the plumed look: *on this page* is a hat and veil made entirely from feathers, with brightly coloured tips.

BV 1946 Eric.
Reboux

B V 1948 John Deakin. *Aage Thaarup*

A V 1947 Frances McLaughlin. *Lilly Daché*

A V 1948 Frances McLaughlin. *Lilly Daché*

Tabletalk. Will the large or the small hat win the day at the end of the forties? Wide hats – such as that *on the right*, a big, black Milan straw, and, *above left*, a navy felt oval lined with white and veiled – were worn, but were much more formal than the picture hats which the New Look had brought. Generally, smaller hats were smarter, in keeping with the tailored look of fashion, like the black-veiled white hat, *opposite*, and the black velours, *above right*. Fashionable colours were stark contrasts, navy and white, black and white.

A V 1948 Penn. *Irene*

1950

Wide hat reminiscent of a nun's headdress. FV 1953 Henry Clarke. *Albouy*

The sou'wester: in fine straw *above,* Swiss Braid *below.* BV 1957 Henry Clarke. *Simone Mirman.* AV 1956 John Stewart. *Emme*

During the fifties fashion reached a watershed. The sculptured clothes of the early part of the decade, emphasizing the curves of the body underneath, stabilized fashion after the turmoil of the war. Newly returned, too, was the fun of being able to wear a great variety of different styles and colours in clothes and accessories. *Vogue* showed small, stark hats described as 'emphatically feminine', although clothes and hat together created an aggressive and uncompromising look.

Until the late 1950s, the hat had often determined the accompanying outfit. Despite wartime difficulties in manufacture and availability of materials, hats in the early forties had still been produced and keenly sought after, for they were often the one bright note among the dull clothes available. During the fifties, however, the role of hats changed quietly but vitally. They became one element of the overall image, milliners following the look for the season in both clothes and accessories. The young started to react against fashion's orientation towards an age group of twenty-five plus: new designers appeared, producing ready-to-wear young sports clothes and teenage fashions, and a new type of shop emerged to sell them. Young women began also to resent the necessity to have a different hat for every occasion, indeed to wear a hat at all. Initiative in hat design slackened as Couture millinery, which had the most scope for creating new designs, became less influential, less patronized.

The smart hats of the early fifties were very varied, but all alluring, tipped back to reveal the brow, yet leaving the back of the head exposed. The large picture hats of 1950 had rigid brims and low crowns, appliqué flowers, ribbon edging. By 1952 crowns were smaller still, brims dipping on either side of the head, or swept up at the front in a sort of half-Breton, with the brim tapering away at the back: a characteristic look of the mid-fifties. The sides of the larger hat, on a downward curve since the outset of the decade, were now at times completely separated, producing a shape oddly reminiscent of a nun's winged headdress. Smaller hats, in straws, velours (favourite fabric of 1953) and felt, were perched on top of backcombed, but neatly pinned up, or rolled hair. Shapes varied: some were sharply angular, some shell-shaped, slightly rounded, all stark in either cut or colour. Evening hats were 'more than a coiffure, less than a hat', tiny clusters of feathers, or masses of ostrich feathers forming a soft brim around a pillbox. 'An extravagant note assures the success of evening hats', said *Vogue*. The feather 'wig', popular in the forties, was still worn. Some hats, chosen to match specific clothes in cut and colour, were lined with identical fabric. Often veiled, the coarse silk variety was the most popular, always accompanied by a pair of slanting, black-lashed eyes.

Milliners in the mid-fifties looked to the past for inspiration, producing nostalgic quasi-Edwardian hats, boaters. For evening a huge black hat, rigidly constructed with wide, high crown and wide brim, could be laden with white fur, or for daytime, lighter versions were wound with ribbon, covered with full-blown roses. 'The most important hat news', said *Vogue*, '. . . is the heavy-headed flowered hat . . . the more-hat idea.' The less-hat movement was also gaining force: *Vogue* was full of tiny round velvet circles masquerading as pillboxes or turbans for day and evening. For everyday wear, the hat was a contributing factor in the creation of a look in which make-up played an increasingly important role. 'Whether it's a close but deep-set hat, or deep and wide, it calls for a new look that has all the allure that modern eye make-up can manage.' Eyes were particularly important: during the forties eyelashes had been darkened, but now eyelid colour too was vital. Eyebrows were darkened with a pencil.

During the last four years of the decade, hats began to cover the brow once again. Dior popularized the 'sou'wester', which was created in a variety of fabrics for winter and summer wear. Other shapes were the Breton, wide-brimmed hats with the mannish squared crown, tiny pillboxes on the top of the head or over a high bun, covered in chocolate-box bows and flowers. Many small hats were derived from berets and turbans, with soft draping built into the shape; they were worn on one side of the head. Two interesting shapes were the 'hairdryer hat', pinned to the highest point of the raised hair, framing the head in fine black stiffened tulle, and a hat like a rugby ball. This appeared in fine and rough straws, heavily topstitched to give it texture. Veils were still highly fashionable. 'Evening hats', said *Vogue*, 'are the new and dramatic arrival in the world of after dark'; they were frivolous, small, large, flowery, feathery, or merely a huge satin bow. Sports hats were now, almost traditionally, velours or felt in a feminine trilby.

Swirls of tulle, clusters of net and veiling, were all popular throughout the decade, used in various ways. Veiling might reach the eyes, or fasten at the back of the neck, completely covering the head. Straws were used, including Swiss Braid and varnished coarse varieties, which produced textured effects. Black hats were smartest during the early fifties; later colours were orange, red, yellow. 'The coming hat colour,' said *Vogue* in 1956, 'is violet, a shade that operates superbly with everything but black.' Now large hats were ornamented with fabric flowers, singly, but most often in clusters. Provençal or Oriental flower prints, on cotton or silk, were an alternative to the ever-popular straws. In the second half of the decade velvet and tweed were used to match suits and coats. Evening hats used all the exotica: silk, satin, velvet, paste jewels (to match paste earrings), straight and curled feathers galore, tassels, flowers. But despite lively evening hats, the excitement of millinery was on the decline. 'People say,' said French *Vogue* in 1959, 'that Parisiennes no longer wear hats. Sadly, this has some truth in it.'

The less-hat movement: tiny velvet circle. F V 1952 Rawlings. *Christian Dior*

Evening hat perched on backcombed hair. A V 1956 Frances McLaughlin. *Adolfo of Emme*

1960

VOGUE

A V 1950 Penn.
Lilly Daché

**The Black and
White Idea**

London Season

Two big, black
alluring hats
from 1950.
Severely cut, like
the clothes worn
with them, they
are veiled for a
touch of
mystery. The
bicorne skimmer,
opposite, wings
up at the back to
show off the
new, short
haircut. On
Vogue's only
black-and-white
cover, *this page*, a
low-crowned,
wide hat worn
very flat, with
scarf tied under
the chin.

B V 1950 Penn.
Lilly Daché

JUNE 1950

BV 1953 Bouché.
Agmar

New, sleek sports cars command headgear. The Bouché cover, *opposite*, shows a white helmet hood in suede-finish jersey with ribbing to frame the face, worn by the driver of a brand new Austin-Healey Hundred. *On this page*, one of the first Daimler Conquest Roadsters, so speedy that it necessitated this linen wind-cap whose shape is reminiscent of twenties hat design.

BV 1955 Norman Parkinson.
Herbert Johnson

FV 1953 Henry Clarke.
Balenciaga

Two Couture hats
in an Edwardian
mood: *on this page*,
a vast black velours
hat laden with
cygnet down, to
wear with a cocktail
dress; *opposite*, a
flying-saucer of a
boater, in natural
straw with simple
black ribbon. Eyes
are now thickly
rimmed with kohl,
lips bright, brows
dark for emphasis
under these huge
brims.

BV 1955 Karen Radkai.
Givenchy

Hats make cover news, *opposite*, six day and evening hats in printed and plain fabrics, with feathers. A turban, little more than a flat bow, *on this page*, in silk taffeta.

Above:
A V 1957 Karen Radkai.
Sally Victor
A V 1957 Penn. *Dior*
A V 1957 Karen Radkai.
Adolfo of Emme
Below:
B V 1956 Henry Clarke.
Paulette
A V 1957 Rawlings.
Sally Victor
A V 1956 Penn. *Mr John*

F V 1959 William Klein.
Gilbert Orcal

BV 1958 Claude Virgin.
Rudolph

Sophisticated dinner hats were a strong fashion note of the late fifties, worn with long, ornate paste earrings, long black gloves. *On this page* is a 'hairdryer hat', a transparent black bell of organdie gathered at the back in a black-leaved, white-petalled rose. Long downy feathers, *opposite*, create a similarly mysterious veiled look, falling from a small fitted cap.

BV 1956 Henry Clarke. *Dior*

BV 1958
Claude Virgin.
Lanvin-Castello

The hat which
Vogue described as
'Ascot's most
beautiful' in 1958,
on this page: a
shallow, curving
sailor made entirely
of net, the brim
tucked and softened,
with a spotted cloud
of veiling. *Opposite*,
a superb scarlet
'rugby-ball' toque.
Parkinson called
this photograph
'Van Dongen', after
that artist's painting
*The Lady Wants No
Children*.

BV 1959
Norman Parkinson.
Otto Lucas

1960

Hatted heads were far less common in the sixties than in the previous decade. Fashion's emphasis was on girls in their teens and early twenties, who wanted lighthearted fashions of their own. In previous decades women had worn hats because etiquette and fashion demanded it, apart from any personal considerations. Now, for all but very formal occasions, hats were an optional extra worn for amusement, because they were eye-catching, stylish, and flattering. Fashion was informal, fun, leaving behind the rather set, calculated look of the fifties. 'Every day and in every way you can be different and different and different,' said *Vogue*, and indeed fashion changed its mood from day to day, from 'little girl' to 'unisex' to 'romantic': hats had to be able to cope with this. Hairstyles augmented the informality of millinery, for however formal a hat might be, it could not remain so when perched atop the 'beehive', or any backcombed, curled styles with tendrils of hair escaping around the hat's edges. These untidy hairstyles were a rebellion against the regimented shapes of earlier decades, when etiquette had dictated that hair under hats had to be controlled, however long and curly it might be.

For milliners, the sixties heralded bad times. Fewer women bought hats, and those that did wore the same hat for a variety of occasions which might once have commanded separate styles of their own. Daytime hats could be adapted for evening, like the type which *Vogue* noted could be jogged into evening by the addition of a rose and veiling. Young women wanted cheap, bright hats which they could buy with clothes in the new boutiques, rather than in traditional milliners' shops. Fewer women were prepared to pay the price of a model hat. The simple shapes now in demand often varied only in colour and fabric, and thus were increasingly mass produced.

The most outstanding change in hat shapes during the early sixties was in the sudden growth of the crown. Partly because of the fashion for high, full hairstyles, the increasing size of the crown, and later of the brim, created the sixties top-heavy, doll-like look. Pale lips and make-up, long dark false eyelashes all added to the illusion. The fashionable sou'wester-shaped hat had a tall, broad crown and wide brim; the coolie hat ran brim and crown together. Both these shapes were popular in such diverse materials as straws (for example Swiss Braid), horsehair, ribbed jersey, tweed, felt. Like the hairstyles under them, these hats 'tilt back to leave the brow clear, but sleekily framed . . . the biggest hats are blowing up in the wake of the collections'. For summer, crownless versions appeared, freeing the hair to rise as high as fashion decreed. Smaller shapes, too, cone-shaped hats with turnback brims, the sixties-style 'cloche', and 'caps', a term used now for small shapes: casquettes, toques, boaters, soft berets on brims.

Horticultural hats were the excitement of the early sixties: 'the hat that's a flower . . . like putting your head in an enormous chrysanthemum.' One of

The mannish look: black bowler and cigar. A V 1968 Penati

Chrysanthemum of a hat, in silk. A V 1960 Rutledge. *Adolfo of Emme* the most stunning, a vast flower-head, each petal a tube of silk, was fastened to the crown with clusters of lily of the valley. Others were covered in tiny flowers, or appliquéd with flower shapes. This 'natural' texture theme was continued by widespread use of feathers and fur. The fur 'halo hat' in long-haired skins like red fox was popular, as was the hood which appeared in 1962, made from pink, curly ostrich feathers. These natural materials created a substantial, but soft, silhouette, which was the desired look for smart heads. Shapes were very simple, all attention being channelled into colour and texture.

By the middle of the decade hairstyles were inclining to high spirals, top knots, plaits, short styles, hairpieces added. British *Vogue* noted that hats, in keeping, were 'notable for size and flattery: immense haloes, soft capelines, tiny toques or bun caps.' Dior produced a 'crazy cartwheel'; Saint Laurent, a 'square-brimmed hat', an oversized boater; Givenchy, a flattering chignon hat, vertically fixed to the back of the hair, plumage cascading from it. These couturier hats were sophisticated, aimed at women past their teens, but the shapes were later translated into the more casual form that teenagers wanted. Wide-brimmed hats in bright prints, felt, soft straws, were all very popular, but with soft, floppy brims which framed the face just as satisfactorily as the fashionable hoods or scarves. Among smaller hats, berets were the most popular, sometimes crocheted, in bright colours, worn at any angle.

Mannish hats characterize the last years of the sixties. Dior produced the hunting bowler in black velours, for wear with tailored suits: Stetsons and trilbies followed, worn with a variety of casual clothes. The Stetson was usually made from matt felt, the trilby in tweeds, plaid, sometimes with veiling attached. Versatile and 'unisex', these shapes were widely worn. The major alternative to the mannish look was 'romantic – in the way you widen your eyes when you wear a big-brimmed hat'. Romantic hats were often large, in flower-covered straw, lace or broderie anglaise, or with fringed brim. Smaller-brimmed versions sometimes had softly bloused crowns, complemented by soft-focus eye make-up.

Textured fabrics were the most popular for hats during most of the decade. Furs – ocelot, mink, fox, all the fakes, particularly leopardskin – were popular for toques, halo hats, trilbies, even little-girl hoods. Feathers, too, were used to create hats, but rarely as trimming. Ribbed jersey, crochet, knitted fabric, brushed velours, coarse Swiss Braid, check and fleck tweed, lace, broderie anglaise, all gave hats unusual surface effects.

Some simple straws were decorated with flowers, leaves, lace, but in general the texture of hats made additional ornament unnecessary. American *Vogue* summarized the appeal of contemporary hats quite simply as 'allure: they're steeped in it, with lots of earring, hair, and as many extra eyelashes as can be batted comfortably'.

Furlined hood to frame the face.
BV 1961 Penn.

Textured straw, low over the eyes.
BV 1964 Traeger. *Simone Mirman*

1970

BV 1967 David Bailey.

Two of the strongest looks of the
sixties demonstrate how hats had
become optional extras worn for fun,
to add the finishing touch to a
colour-linked ensemble. *Left*, Saint
Laurent uses the same Abraham
printed silk to link hat and dress: the
print – stylized flowers and leaves –
and the stitching on the soft-brimmed
'cloche' are both characteristic of the
decade. Another example of the
'psychedelic' look, *opposite*, in a riot
of Latin-American flamenco ruffles,
nineteenth-century 1968, with huge
straw hat to echo the shape of the
layered petticoat, peasant scarf
beneath. The black and white outfit,
above, is in quite a different mood.
The small Stetson is one of the
traditionally male hat shapes which
were adapted for female use during
the sixties.

BV 1967 David Bailey.
Saint Laurent

BV 1968 David Bailey.
Gérard Pipart at Nina Ricci

V 1963
David Bailey.
James Wedge

The high hairstyles
of the early sixties
led the way to
higher crowns for
hats. The simple
shape of a school-
girl's hat, *opposite*,
was a popular one
throughout the
decade; here
covered in soft
white feathers, with
a ping-pong ball for
a dove's egg. Suzy
Parker, *on this page*,
in Otto Lucas' shop,
wears the sou'wester
hat which first came
into fashion during
the late fifties,
remaining fashion-
able with still deeper
crown until the
mid-sixties.

BV 1962
Henry Clarke.
Otto Lucas

V 1969
avid Bailey.
tto Lucas

Naturally textured
hats: a halo of silver
fox, *opposite*,
simplest shape to
show off the fur's
colours and texture.
On this page, a huge
toque of Mongolian
lamb, worn
informally over
flowing hair, with a
coat lined to
co-ordinate.

BV 1968
Barry Lategan.
Otto Lucas

BV 1967 Jeanloup Sieff. *Herbert Johnson*

The tailored, mannish look of the late sixties, with hat shapes stolen from male wardrobes. Models and their lifelike copies, *left*, all wear versatile black felt Stetsons: in a military mood, *far left*, or merely as wet-weather gear, *near left*. A dog-tooth check tweed suit, *above*, contrasts with the beige bloomed velvet soft-brimmed cone, trimmed with tiny pheasant feathers, and worn with a feathery-knit brown balaclava underneath.

BV 1968 Helmut Newton. *Herbert Johnson*

A V 1968 Patrick Lichfield.
Adolfo

A V 1968 Patrick Lichfield. *Adolfo*

Romantic hats for summer days
spent lolling in flower-filled fields,
dressed in flowing layers of white
lawn, ruffled broderie anglaise: a
sixties interpretation of Edwardian
summertime. *Left and above*, two
vast white summer straws covered
with eyelet, with or without
ruffles, worn with hair left loose.
Opposite, the soft velours black
Tyrolean hat is rendered romantic
by ringlets and fresh country
flowers.

A V 1967 Franco Rubartelli.
Archie Eason

1970

Felt hat with 'pop' appliqué. FV 1970
Pull-on almost-cloche. BV 1977
Willie Christie. *Graham Smith/Harrods*

'Farewell folklore and fantasy disguises,' said French *Vogue* in 1971, 'real women are back in fashion. The new mode is a hymn to civilized womanhood, to the woman who is soignée to the tips of her red fingernails.' This new mood in fashion immediately dated the fashions of the sixties, which were, by comparison, stylized, naive, wooden. The look now was a very individual one, no longer breathlessly dependent on tracking down the latest 'pop' accessory, but on a personal interpretation of designer looks. The rebellion of the fifties and sixties was over. A new régime began to be established, ready-to-wear and Couture operating side by side, with little hostility. Clothes emphasized the body, which was, ideally, slender, fit, energetic. Throughout the decade clothes were supple, practical and comfortable. At first they were layered: coat over waistcoat, over jumper, over shirt, with skirt, thick tights, leg-warmers, stout shoes, hat and scarf, in soft fabrics and knits; later the look was pared down. Separates were still a key factor, but dresses became more important too; as *Vogue* said, 'less is more', advocating no-fuss clothes. For evening there were extravagances in luxury fabrics, with a Victorian feel and still a touch of the Orient.

During this decade a new breed of 'soft-wear' hats was in fashion. Although rooted in previous millinery moods, they were new both in the suppleness of fabrics used, allowing the hat to mould to the head, and in the natural way in which they were worn. Neither casual nor formal, everyday hats (which were not worn *every* day) were worn as part of an outfit, not as a last-minute addition. Hairstyles were still long, straight and 'hippy' at the beginning of the seventies, credited in *Vogue* as 'hair combed by . . .'. Long curls became fashionable, and by the second half of the decade hairdressers had never been busier, as the craze for blow-drying, rather than roller-drying, left the haircut very much on display, with or without a hat.

Hats in the early seventies had high, rounded crowns, big brims draping softly around the face. Many were made from felt, in a wide range of colours, others from coarse or fine straw. Up-to-date notes were stars, hearts, halfmoons – all the 'pop' symbols appliquéd on hats as on shoes; or else scarves and shawls in flower-print paisley wrapped round the crown. Wide summer and party hats often had lavish, jokey, dotted or speckled veiling and feathers, and were worn with paste drop earrings. Smaller hats, too, were veiled, as a retro forties look became fashionable, carried through with antique clothes to match, bought in antique and street markets, which had become a source of fashionable clothes since the sixties. *Vogue* described one of these retro hats as 'an uncompromising pillbox tipped over one eyebrow', advising its readers to 'get used to it now before anyone else'. The look was not widely popular at the time, but was intermittently adopted throughout the decade, particularly for festive and evening wear. The hat which really did shape the whole decade's heads was what American *Vogue* first described as 'the mushroom cap to plop on your head' in crushed suede. It was an almost-cloche, its crown not quite deep enough to merit the full title, in fabric with topstitched brim, or in felt. Immensely versatile, it could be worn with brim turned down or up, with various hairstyles, could be worn through the day and into early evening. In its simplest felt form, it was so cheap that women could own the same hat in a variety of colours.

Knitted and crocheted hats were fashionable throughout the first half of the decade. At first heavy, in thick rib wool or crocheted cotton, they matched scarves, jumpers, gloves: designers created a whole outfit in the same knitted look. Later they were made from finer knits, cashmere, lambs-wool, fine wool jersey, with cuffed edge, pulled down all around the head. 'If you want a new thing to put on your head' wrote *Vogue* in 1976, 'it's the scarf-wrapped head.' Scarves, turbans, with glitter-threads and embroidery, in Oriental and flower prints, were wound around the head, knotted or plaited. The twenties look was revived again as a result of the appearance of *The Great Gatsby* on film; this era had already undergone one revival in the mid-sixties. Once again beaded caps were the rage for parties.

The last years of the seventies, like the late fifties, were an uncertain time for the hat. Active sports were more fashionable than ever, new hats were designed, for example, for ski-ing, but in many cases women looked to traditional shapes for sporting headgear, produced by sportswear companies. Hats for special occasions were broad, shallow-crowned straws, or small neat pillboxes trimmed with flowers or veiling. For evening and smart daytime wear there were flat plates of varnished straw to be worn at a rakish angle at the side of a swept-up hairstyle, or tiny caps which were sequinned, or covered in flowers. Hats were, now, really worn for fun. Fewer women than ever before wore them, as fashion adopted an informal, bareheaded look.

Felt was the most widely used fabric for hats in the early seventies, in a huge variety of colours, trimmed with leather thongs, studs, appliqué pop shapes. It was used for the huge hats of the opening years, alongside fine straws, and later for the pull-on, narrow-brimmed hats popular for most of the decade, for berets. Tweeds and plaids for flat caps, velvet and cord for pull-on hats are all characteristic of the mid-seventies. Most popular of all were knitted and crocheted hats: coarse, fine, furry or plain, patterned or random-coloured, in soft earth tones, or brighter mauves, greens, reds. Pattern-woven straws, furs, sequins, beads, were all used for hats.

Amusement value was still the prime attribute of early eighties hats in *Vogue*. But the fact that the head was attracting a great deal of fashion emphasis, adorned with masses of dishevelled, well-highlighted hair, ribbons and lace bands, implied a not-too-distant return to the hat. As fashion took a more serious turn, too, towards sophisticated, tailored clothes, hats became the natural finishing touch.

Retro pillbox with seductive veiling. BV 1972 Bourdin. *Karl Lagerfeld*

Country cap. FV 1975 Hans Feurer

1980

BV 1974 Barry Lategan.
Outlander

Knitted hats were highly
fashionable during the early
seventies. The hat, *left*, is
part of a whole ensemble in
the same variegated yarn
which was a popular type; others
were slubbed, or fine
cashmere and lambswool.
The same neat silhouette
was created by the scarf-
wrapped head: Twiggy,
opposite, wears a purply-
brown, rather twenties
version.

BV 1973 Justin de
Villeneuve. *Biba*

Many hats were worn
just for fun during the
early seventies, when
there was great
uncertainty as to the
future of the hat. Crazy
hat with two crowns
(and crazy 3-D fabrics
for dresses), just for
fun, *opposite*. Fulfilling
a serious protective
function are the two
soft felts, *this page*,
single versions of the
hat *opposite*, with
bright fabric ties.

FV 1971 Guy Bourdin.
Jean-Charles Brosseau

AV 1971 Renati. *Adolfo*

Veils were used in various ways by milliners during the seventies. The patterned veil, *above*, contrasts with the simple lines of the small cloche, creating a sophisticated whole. At the other end of the decade, *right*, this vast, curving, fine green straw is sophisticated too, but in the current, less formal, style. Fine veiling in matching colour covers the shallow crown and brim, extending over the face.

BV 1978 Albert Watson. *Frederick Fox*

90

V 1974 Barry Lategan.
aint Laurent Rive Gauche

A pull-on felt hat,
opposite, in the style
and fabric most used
in the seventies. With
its narrow brim and
simple crown, this
was a very versatile
shape which was easy
to mass-produce in a
wide variety of
colours at a low price.
For the fashion-
conscious young man,
this page, mummy's
khaki pull-on was
an essential accessory.

Overleaf: holiday hats
made fashion news.
The hat bought in
Guadeloupe, *on the left*,
was equally fashionable
at home. The
musterer's hat, *right*, is
a practical fly-swatter
in the outback, fun
fashion everywhere
else.
B V 1981 Eric Boman
B V 1980 Bruce Weber.
Laurence Corner

B V 1971 Duc

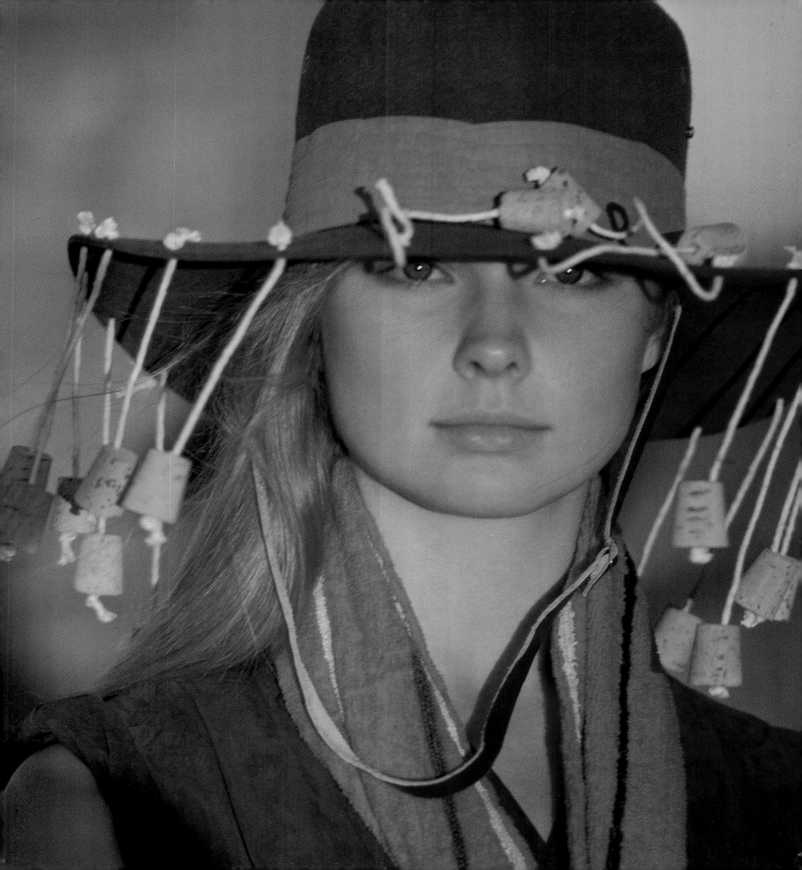

Her Royal Highness, The Princess of Wales, latest royal millinery arbiter, at Sandown Park in a soft trilby. BV 1981 Desmond O'Neill.